BILLY JOEL

T0081655

2 And So It Goes

4 Honesty

7 It's Still Rock and Roll to Me

12 Just the Way You Are

15 The Longest Time

18 Lullabye (Goodnight, My Angel)

20 My Life

26 New York State of Mind

23 Piano Man

30 The River of Dreams

36 She's Always a Woman

33 She's Got a Way

Cover Photo © Clayton Call / Retna Ltd./MediaPunch

ISBN 978-1-4950-3065-9

HAL•LEONARD® CORPORATION
7777 W. Bluemound Rd. P.O. Box 13819 Milwaukee, WI 53213

In Australia Contact:
Hal Leonard Australia Pty. Ltd.
4 Lentara Court
Cheltenham, Victoria, 3192 Australia
Email: ausadmin@halleonard.com.au

For all works contained herein:
Unauthorized copying, arranging, adapting, recording, Internet posting, public performance, or other distribution of the printed music in this publication is an infringement of copyright. Infringers are liable under the law.

Visit Hal Leonard Online at
www.halleonard.com

AND SO IT GOES

Words and Music by
BILLY JOEL

Copyright © 1989 JOELSONGS
This arrangement Copyright © 2016 JOELSONGS
All Rights Administered by ALMO MUSIC CORP.
All Rights Reserved Used by Permission

5
1.
2.
1
4
1

HONESTY

Words and Music by
BILLY JOEL

Copyright © 1978 IMPULSIVE MUSIC
This arrangement Copyright © 2016 IMPULSIVE MUSIC
All Rights Administered by ALMO MUSIC CORP.
All Rights Reserved Used by Permission

To Coda

D.S. al Coda
CODA

IT'S STILL ROCK AND ROLL TO ME

Words and Music by
BILLY JOEL

Copyright © 1980 IMPULSIVE MUSIC
This arrangement Copyright © 2016 IMPULSIVE MUSIC
All Rights Administered by ALMO MUSIC CORP.
All Rights Reserved Used by Permission

f

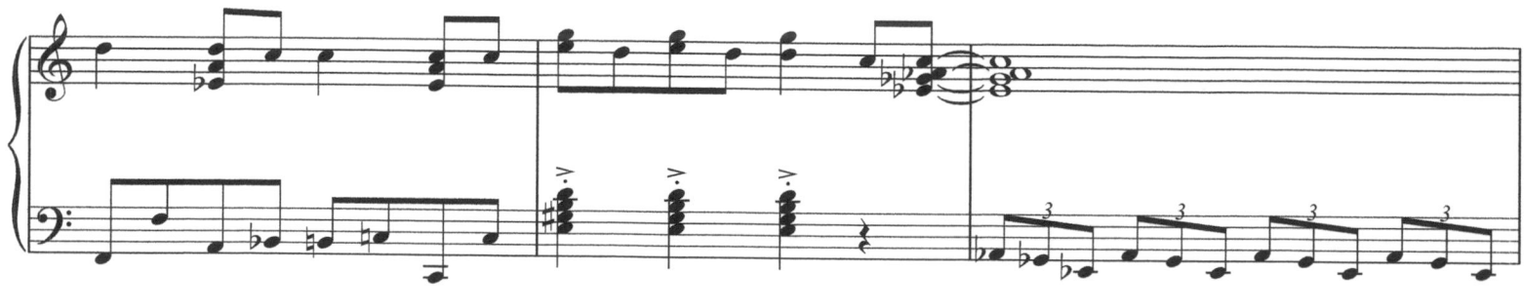

To Coda

D.S. al Coda
CODA

JUST THE WAY YOU ARE

Words and Music by
BILLY JOEL

Copyright © 1977 IMPULSIVE MUSIC
Copyright Renewed
This arrangement Copyright © 2016 IMPULSIVE MUSIC
All Rights Administered by ALMO MUSIC CORP.
All Rights Reserved Used by Permission

To Coda

D.S. al Coda

CODA

THE LONGEST TIME

Words and Music by
BILLY JOEL

Copyright © 1983 JOELSONGS
This arrangement Copyright © 2016 JOELSONGS
All Rights Administered by ALMO MUSIC CORP.
All Rights Reserved Used by Permission

1.
2.

rit.
8vb

LULLABYE
(Goodnight, My Angel)

Words and Music by
BILLY JOEL

Copyright © 1993 IMPULSIVE MUSIC
This arrangement Copyright © 2016 IMPULSIVE MUSIC
All Rights Administered by ALMO MUSIC CORP.
All Rights Reserved Used by Permission

2.
rit.

MY LIFE

Words and Music by
BILLY JOEL

Copyright © 1978 IMPULSIVE MUSIC
This arrangement Copyright © 2016 IMPULSIVE MUSIC
All Rights Administered by ALMO MUSIC CORP.
All Rights Reserved Used by Permission

To Coda
1.
2.

D.S. al Coda
CODA

PIANO MAN

Words and Music by
BILLY JOEL

Copyright © 1973 JOELSONGS
Copyright Renewed
This arrangement Copyright © 2016 JOELSONGS
All Rights Administered by ALMO MUSIC CORP.
All Rights Reserved Used by Permission

1.
2.
rit.

NEW YORK STATE OF MIND

Words and Music by
BILLY JOEL

Copyright © 1976 JOELSONGS
Copyright Renewed
This arrangement Copyright © 2016 JOELSONGS
All Rights Administered by ALMO MUSIC CORP.
All Rights Reserved Used by Permission

To Coda
1.

2.
8va

D.S. al Coda
CODA
rit.
Straight 8ths
p

RIVER OF DREAMS

Words and Music by
BILLY JOEL

Copyright © 1993 IMPULSIVE MUSIC
This arrangement Copyright © 2016 IMPULSIVE MUSIC
All Rights Administered by ALMO MUSIC CORP.
All Rights Reserved Used by Permission

1.
2.

To Coda
D.S. al Coda
(take 2nd ending)
CODA
Freely
8va

SHE'S GOT A WAY

Words and Music by
BILLY JOEL

Copyright © 1971 IMPULSIVE MUSIC
Copyright Renewed
This arrangement Copyright © 2016 IMPULSIVE MUSIC
All Rights Administered by ALMO MUSIC CORP.
All Rights Reserved Used by Permission

1.
2.
𝄋

To Coda

D.S. al Coda
CODA

dim.
rit.
p

SHE'S ALWAYS A WOMAN

Words and Music by
BILLY JOEL

Copyright © 1977 IMPULSIVE MUSIC
Copyright Renewed
This arrangement Copyright © 2016 IMPULSIVE MUSIC
All Rights Administered by ALMO MUSIC CORP.
All Rights Reserved Used by Permission

1.
2.
rit.
pp
8vb

FROM HAL LEONARD

In this series, popular favorites receive unexpected fresh treatments. Uniquely reimagined and crafted for intermediate piano solo, these tunes have been All Jazzed Up!

J.S. BACH
Air on the G String • Aria • Bist du bei mir (Be Thou with Me) • Gavotte • Jesu, Joy of Man's Desiring • Largo • March • Minuet in G • Musette • Sheep May Safely Graze • Siciliano • Sleepers, Awake (Wachet Auf).
00151064 ..... $12.99

THE BEATLES
All My Loving • And I Love Her • Come Together • Eight Days a Week • Eleanor Rigby • The Fool on the Hill • Here, There and Everywhere • Lady Madonna • Lucy in the Sky with Diamonds • Michelle • While My Guitar Gently Weeps • Yesterday.
00172235 ..... $12.99

CHRISTMAS CAROLS
Auld Lang Syne • Deck the Hall • The First Noel • Good King Wenceslas • In the Bleak Midwinter • Jingle Bells • Joy to the World • O Christmas Tree • O Come, All Ye Faithful • O Little Town of Bethlehem • Up on the Housetop • We Wish You a Merry Christmas.
00277866 ..... $12.99

CHRISTMAS SONGS
Blue Christmas • The Christmas Song (Chestnuts Roasting on an Open Fire) • Christmas Time Is Here • Do You Hear What I Hear • Feliz Navidad • Have Yourself a Merry Little Christmas • I'll Be Home for Christmas • Merry Christmas, Darling • Silver Bells • Sleigh Ride • White Christmas • Winter Wonderland.
00236706 ..... $12.99

COLDPLAY
Clocks • Don't Panic • Every Teardrop Is a Waterfall • Fix You • Magic • Paradise • The Scientist • A Sky Full of Stars • Speed of Sound • Trouble • Viva La Vida • Yellow.
00149026 ..... $12.99

DISNEY
Belle • Circle of Life • Cruella De Vil • Ev'rybody Wants to Be a Cat • It's a Small World • Let It Go • Mickey Mouse March • Once upon a Dream • Part of Your World • Supercalifragilisticexpialidocious • Under the Sea • When She Loved Me.
00151072 ..... $14.99

JIMI HENDRIX
Castles Made of Sand • Crosstown Traffic • Fire • Foxey Lady • Hey Joe • Little Wing • Manic Depression • Purple Haze • Spanish Castle Magic • The Wind Cries Mary.
00174441 ..... $12.99

BILLY JOEL
And So It Goes • Honesty • It's Still Rock and Roll to Me • Just the Way You Are • The Longest Time • Lullabye (Goodnight, My Angel) • My Life • New York State of Mind • Piano Man • The River of Dreams • She's Always a Woman • She's Got a Way.
00149039 ..... $12.99

MOTOWN
Ain't Nothing like the Real Thing • How Sweet It Is (To Be Loved by You) • I Can't Help Myself (Sugar Pie, Honey Bunch) • I Heard It Through the Grapevine • I Want You Back • Let's Get It On • My Girl • Never Can Say Goodbye • Overjoyed • Papa Was a Rollin' Stone • Still • You Can't Hurry Love.
00174482 ..... $12.99

NIRVANA
About a Girl • All Apologies • Come as You Are • Dumb • Heart Shaped Box • In Bloom • Lithium • The Man Who Sold the World • On a Plain • (New Wave) Polly • Rape Me • Smells like Teen Spirit.
00149025 ..... $12.99

OZZY OSBOURNE
Crazy Train • Dreamer • Flying High Again • Goodbye to Romance • Iron Man • Mama, I'm Coming Home • Mr. Crowley • No More Tears • Over the Mountain • Paranoid • Perry Mason • Time After Time.
00149040 ..... $12.99

ELVIS PRESLEY
Blue Suede Shoes • Can't Help Falling in Love • Cryin' in the Chapel • Don't • Don't Be Cruel (To a Heart That's True) • Heartbreak Hotel • I Want You, I Need You, I Love You • Jailhouse Rock • Love Me Tender • Suspicious Minds • The Wonder of You • You Don't Have to Say You Love Me.
00198895 ..... $12.99

STEVIE WONDER
As • Ebony and Ivory • For Once in My Life • I Just Called to Say I Love You • I Wish • Isn't She Lovely • My Cherie Amour • Ribbon in the Sky • Signed, Sealed, Delivered I'm Yours • Sir Duke • Superstition • You Are the Sunshine of My Life.
00149090 ..... $12.99

www.halleonard.com

Prices, contents and availability subject to change without notice.

Disney characters and artwork © Disney Enterprises, Inc.